# WONDERBENDER

DIANE WALD

1913 Press
www.1913press.org
1913press@gmail.com

Wonderbender


1913 is a not-for-profit organization, with 501(c)3 status pending.
Contributions to 1913 Press may be tax-deductible.
All correspondence & contributions are welcome.

Manufactured in the oldest country in the world, The United States of America.
Many thanks to all the artists, from this century and the last, who made
this project possible.

*This publication is supported in generous part by individual donors:*
Anonymous (9), Robert J. Bertholf, Ectopistes Migratorius, Coco Owen,
Marjorie Perloff, Jean Jacques Poucel, Matvei Yankelevich.



Great thanks to California State University-San Marcos & George Mason University
for their generous support.

***Founder & Editrice***: Sandra Doller
***Designer & Vice-editor***: Ben Doller

Text is set in Dante, titles in Code Light.

***Author Photo:*** P. Carey Reid

***Acknowledgments:***
Some of these poems have appeared in:
*Caprice, Antioch Review, Fence, Ploughshares, Laurel Review, College English, American Poetry Review, Big Bridge, papertiger, MiPoesias, Pleiades, Conduit, Black Warrior Review, Massachusetts Review, Cape Discovery Anthology, 180 More: Extraordinary Poems for Daily Life, Cervena Barva Press postcard series, Court Green, 1913 a journal of forms*

**ISBN-10: 0-9779351-8-3**
**ISBN-13: 978-0-9779351-8-5**

19
13

# WONDERBENDER

# CONTENTS

*for Robert "Early James" Wald*

# THE LARK GAME

what is happening is that the parameters are widening
are shrinking
are moving in and outwards
are changing colors changing shades of colors
and changing the dots of colons
and the bottom commas of semicolons
and while we talk of the same things we are older we are different
others are different

a lark on the wing with a lark in its mouth

there is no red six there is no red seven

# A SILENT WIND OVER THE ISLET

I'd forgotten you so liked art. And many things
advanced in those days to a point of consciousness
beyond any speech or understanding
the nerves could utter. Yet when I designed
the fine-blown glassware you impressed
upon each piece a delicate leaf, a hand,
a monstrous kiss that marked each one's
relief from the next, an individual differing
so slightly from its kin, but greatly,
that every one-celled stem
floated its flower-house into a globe, a fishbowl end,
resting at last at level on the table.

Tigers love water. They sleep with their heads
towards the outside wall, and write with blue chalk
on the sidewalk. Outside blue. Eagerly I hand over
the lights to you, but soundless now,
as the man with his ear to the floor must be disowned
and drowned and downed by the giant. Once
you healed a woman twice. The color teal. The crayfish
glimmering in still pools and insect wings
of mica. And the hush. The awful stars. It all
comes back to me now in a wind-up of clouds
as softly they fall to your tie, to your shoulders.

How shall we move from one height to the next
except by the dark back stairs? A wooden linkage
creaks, a figure moves in violets and regrets,
pressing its face to the wall along the steps
so that the dreamers on the other side can hear
the contours of a presence at once kind and cold.
I remember you loved the hour without name

and every shade behind the purchased mask
with both its mouths. The clocks we found
moved backwards, moved in unison once a year,
and we've survived that moment in the mirror
as amber acquaintances. In the very end
you will be made to speak of me, you will
entirely forget, in every case, the distance
from the liquid to the rim, And you will then
believe we really did all the things we imagined.

# I CALLED THE PAINTING *TRISH THE BLUE*

for no good reason. Just knew it should be called that after many nights awake with the worry of death, a drama, having to say it over and over and over again, I will not die this time, having to trust someone to take care of me, and the postcard of the painting too and also my cats, some books, a little clothing. The painting isn't mine, I came across it on a desk somewhere, found it was one of those things you could fall right into, the layers of color so clear, so all-around-you. Down in one corner, the left I think, some locks of a yellowish fear, but then they dissolved upwards into the self of Trish the Blue. It was she, Trish, who helped me. "Set down this worry," she said, "and look into me. Listen to no one else; they will confuse you." I looked far in. There was peace there. There was lavender, there was green, there were halos for me and a few good friends. I saw that I could believe her. I took a breath.

# CAROLINA WREN

do i want to go to prague? maybe.

it is always a matter of lunch with clotheslines.

these small things we need.

my husband asks if i am 'on schedule.'

we consult with his sister about the subjunctive.

in two languages.

and then this morning i am stunned by my forgetfulness, stunned by the surge of botanicals, appalled in general by the suffusion of memories that drowns my forgetfulness, by the memory of profusion and the doubtfulness therein. i love you and i hide from you. of that i can be certain.

i am offended by the depth of my sleep, sleep that is like a deep fall into a deep sweet cavern, and the cavern lined in velvet. the velvet is dark, but it is not black. there is a sheen to the velvet like the shaved spot on the skin of the cat who receives medical treatment. the tenderest spot, the spot steeped in sleepiness of touch. i am intrigued by the depth of my sleep and the condition of my bones when i wake. bones like marshmallow, bones like iron. the iron and the marshmallow fighting. nobody wins.

the day before yesterday i spotted a carolina wren, ascertained its identity in three bird identification books. it has not returned since. it flew from the feeder three times on a direct diagonal to the small green birdhouse on the crab-cherry tree. if there is such a thing. the man who was hired to treat the tree for fungus has been fired. he will not disturb the bird.

and i have written a note to a favorite author to see if she would like some advice. will she answer? and i have written a note to dead james and to dead garth and to dead grace and to dead allen; i have written these notes in my head only, and, like notes that go often to god, they are asking favors. when i cease to ask favors my notes will be answered. i have not written my father or mother.

odd how the spaces look different when they're always the same.

odd how you wait for me to speak.

odd how i do it.

# THE USE OF HYPNOSIS MAY SEEM TO PROMISE A SOLUTION

but it does not
perceptions are constructions of phenomena and memories reconstructions of constructions
an unreliable method of establishing truth in telling
truth in untelling
untruth untelling truthfully
what is your suggestion?
we now recognize that as untrue
possibly
i am by my very nature *varyingly veridical* i have
veridical hallucinations which do in fact coincide with some crisis
but which almost never identify clearly
the life of the person whose image is seen on the screen

it may have been young cathy t
who was older when i met her

and i draw human characters the most veridically
when my poetical delineator
is out of order

so veridicality is the degree of correspondence between a remembered or imagined situation and
a version of that event that can be verified by some accepted correlative source

amen

when there is no such external source the potential for correlation or even of triangulation
is lacking
and we have to accept the high degree of uncertainty present in our

observations.

so often we simply cannot decide

i am wondering if you will discover my miracle
the veridical hallucinations of a myriad of ancestral tones
played on a child's harp
in the woods on a rainy tuesday

it was summer
it was new jersey
it was winter and it was not

the veridicality of the imagination of some writers

some writers like me

most likely cannot be trusted
i mean i'd be careful if i were you i'd just be careful
not paranoid but aware
if you know what i mean

i advise caution on these matters of external facts
as we are so used in most situations to asking direct questions to get at the actual answers
and this is the most unreliable method although we have
an understandable prejudice in favor of tangible and concrete external data

you must squelch this nasty tendency
really if you want to get anywhere

also it's hard to remember what not to say
when you have dreamed it
even with all the current evidence we simply do not know
which dreams are lying

and which lies are true

our earliest most loved and most feared figures
must be questioned
and their experience correlated with others
so that we may suspend our certainty and look inwards as well as outwards

we suffer all opinions prematurely
but the facts can spoil a good story
and describing these stories to an interested objective other
helps us gradually to approach veridicality
in the manner in which we get dressed up in our softest clothes
and approach each other calmly

to be kissed

we make better approximations of reality
if we try to climb into the quarry
than if we sit on the edge with a picnic
looking down

but so much of the past and even the present
remains uncertain in our lives even after a lengthy appraisal
like this memory i suffer of a hot summer day
with my shoulders blistered
being forced to sing a song

this may be a self-serving imaginative construction
or not
there simply is no telling.

*do you hear that bird?*
*do you hear that summer bird?*

it's a meadowlark yellow as a bean i do remember
and meadowlarks don't usually come in yellow

# FORTUNE COOKIES

** The stars appear every night in the sky.*
*All is well.**

If you should become happy
you must let me know. For over forty years
you have carried your life
like a heavy package
you never thought to open.

**Because of your melodic nature, the*
*moonlight never misses an appointment.**

Your wife returns today
from a month-long trip
and you drive through the snow to meet her.

She would like you to greet her
as the person you are in her dreams,
the person you were when you knew she was no one else,
the person who sang in the moonlight
in his natural lonely high voice.

**Very often you cannot help*
*thinking of somebody.**

Always you are thinking
of somebody else. Always.
The moonlight, therefore,
misses its appointment.

When the stars appear every night in the sky
you don't notice that all is well.

# GREEN SHOULDERPAD

Was it someone swimming alongside the rowboat
that made you remember? The color of the water: green,
sliced jade, flipping off the hands of the swimmer
like so many rings. He was unknown to you,
that swimmer, or known only as someone very skilled,
his face almost unseen unless it tipped
near you, as the head turned with the arms.
Precarious. As when the other got into your heart
like an x-ray, burdening you with the knowledge
that *prodigal* did not mean *returning*,
but *recklessly wasteful*. You did not
agree with that, and yet it's true, as far
as truth-in-language goes. It upset you
out of a childhood yarn, wherein the swimmer
climbed onto the raft, and disappeared.

And when you disembarked, on the little island,
you saw a tiny eggshell float
among the flat jade leaves of waterlilies.
You remembered the feel of the green shoulderpad
that time that you dislodged it from his coat
with an embrace. Accidental,
and he took it off to sew. As accidental as the embrace,
or as the eggshell, which you picked up, feeling
as though you'd slept too long. Half an eggshell,
I should have said; you imagined the other half
shattered, or acquired by someone else. The brownish streaks
would not wash off; they seemed to be a part
of the design. Into your pocket, and you thought,
*"What happened to the tiny bird is moot: it flew off,*
*or it died, and probably I*
*will never know the difference."*

# WOMAN FEEDING SPARROW BY HAND

First, that is not the name of the bird. The name of the bird is Jen. And the woman is not so much feeding the bird Jen as allowing her to take a black seed from her hand. Or Jen is allowing the woman to offer her the seed.

The sun is bright; the woman has noticed that when the sun is bright, Jen, or other birds just like her, consent to feed. The woman wears sunglasses so she can see Jen clearly.

A reflection from the sunglasses sometimes frightens Jen. Sometimes she (Jen) flies off with a seed only to find it's hollow. Then she must fly back. Make another selection.

The woman's husband is watching from the window. It is he who has taught her to feed birds by hand. He has not met Jen; or, in truth, they can't be certain.

The sun begins setting around four o'clock. Late January. Snow glistening in the air. A fine mist of glass comes down on the woman and Jen. The grapevines need pruning.

The photograph closes.

# THE VERSIONER

I tell you I'm going to write a poem called "The Versioner" based on what
you said
about yourself at the reading and you say
"Please do." I do write one. Then I remember
That you also said you were "a slanter," but decide not to do
much of anything with that. Then later
in the afternoon I become rather suddenly
fatigued, stretch out on the old foldaway couch
with a blanket and a cat and a silly movie from the sixties
which starts out looking as if it will be insulting to women
but ends up with the male lead saying to the female lead "I love you in spite
of the fact
that you've become beautiful," so all
is well. You have been stealthily slanting, I suppose,
for years, but I did not know. Or I knew it, but it was somewhat elusive,
like the blue in the center of Motherwell's 1969 *Blue Elegy*
which all three of us see in the museum and which one of us says contains
"electric blue." I know what he means—that the blue is quivering or
excited, but it is not really "electric blue," any more than
grass is electric green. It's got more turquoise in it than that and even
turquoise
is wrong, by a long shot. I knew you were slanting but it was too personal
to approach, although it was standing right behind me at the sink
as I ground cold beans for coffee. It was standing right
next to me—leaning along my side in fact—while I tried to decipher
the fifth photograph to the right of the second one by Cameron
on the second floor. The midnight galactic cafe was closed, alas. The light
was too dim in the Japanese gallery but the tile floors gleamed
supernaturally in the small room with the cast-iron horse. It reminded me
of the mirrored Paris room of Rodin, or the crazy bedroom Gaudí designed
for the cigarette girl in Milan. I wasn't there. The theme song played long
in the silly movie and I began to realize it wasn't so silly at all, for both the
duet
being explained by the music and the woman's bow-shaped mouth

had a depth of harmony that nearly silenced the gray inanity
I had somehow been forced to expect. A supporting cast began to discuss
the merits of what was known in other ages
as "courtly love," where the parties in question eschewed all physical contact
in exchange for a deeper, undeniable, brain-woven, heart-directed bond
that did not break, that could not be screeched over
even if the parties took husbands or wives, had children, or
sang different songs. And some of them owned harpsichords, but others
held
guitars. I suppose in some cases the courtlier lovers might fade
right out of the picture, or get painted over
by some less lofty set of sighs, but not in all. Most last
forever. That's a version of truth. That
is a slant on the side of a shadow but still a great deal closer
to some kind of blue than the story you told of A and B and C and D,
with A having a baby that might have belonged
to any of them, but saying that she
was certain the child's real father was D, and then maybe thirty
years later becoming a little dismayed
when you brought it all up. Or you didn't exactly do that—all you actually
said (you said) was "C told me
everything." I imagined
a playful tone. Poor A was quite bollixed. The subject was changed.
A runaway golf cart roared down the road
tippled with tints of lost families. And as for me,
I took some aspirin and slid again downstairs to discuss
what I really meant when I said such-and-such
regarding the stories you told. In the hallway my transplanted lantern
brought in from the garden for winter
made ghostly glows.

# PERISHED GADABOUT

i asked him what the problem was and he said:

*i have been reading. i have been reading the most dismal accounts of vacations in sunny places. also i have this feeling, unaccountably, that there are people i do not know who wrote these accounts and who i will never be able to like. i do not know about their hats, their parents, or their moral habits, and yet i am sure i will not like them. i do not like them now.*

he said:

*the priest came in and showed us the relics: sixteen toes of saint glossolalia,, nineteen arms of saint anapestus, saint poblermane's twelve white breasts, three precious foreskins from the baby jesus, nine whole and complete bodies of saint wally (though his corpse had been cremated), and one petrified tonsil of mary the mother of god—the only piece left when her body ascended to heaven. he told us that relic-seekers were an especially interesting breed.*

and he said: *i have perished as a gadabout*

*i am no longer who i thought i was or would be but i am my own puzzle. everything i say is a surprise to me and an albatross. i have no wingspan nevertheless. the best things i say are flown in an instant and the worst tag behind me. i drag them everywhere.*

he said he was sorry. that there was no news.
that he would not be good company today.

# ONE THING YOU HAVE NEVER (DREAM OF THE REALTORS)

one thing you have never
been is sweet
not sweet so i could tell you
my dream last night of the realtors
who sold me people from the past
disguised as houses

4:45 in the morning here
almost 1:00 p.m. in baghdad
which the radio continues to remind me
although it does not dare predict the suffering of the sand
as it covers the bodies and slurps up the pain of the wounded
the sand absorbing blood and lymph
carrying it swiftly down into the earth
as i lie here dreaming of realtors

i keep going back to the kiss in that dream
the kiss of the realtor
who sold me that girl from fifth grade
and even though she was disguised as a tudor mansion
with espaliered pears along the fence in the yard
i could tell she was all grown up now but with the same hairdo and nose
even though in real life those things had been changed

then there was the kiss of the second realtor who tried
to pretend he was you
he was dressed up like a person
with a keen sense of color
i had a keen sense of distress
at being once again bamboozled

also in the dream i needed to look at some pictures

here is c.k. who changed his name
and whose former wife once told me she'd seen aliens arrive
at her window in new jersey
she was crazy
but not because of the aliens
who may or may not have arrived

and not because of c.k. with his hair of butter and vinegar
and not (perhaps) because of her father who ran the orchestra
but because of her lies and a thought that arrived unexpectedly in the
background
of all the noise she was constantly making
a thought like a rabbit you think that you love
who later turns out to be plastic

suddenly during the dream i understand completely
that i cannot be everywhere at once
and am pulled back in mind to the bookstore shelf
behind the boring sarcastic pompous cynical sloppy lecturer
with his greasy hair
where i kept looking at a book cover i thought was interesting
a white-greyish bed with a pink-orangey coverlet that was partly pulled back
and a figure sitting as if just getting up or just about to lie down or
just sitting there for a moment trying
to catch its breath after a sudden realization
or maybe some terrible surprise although the problem looks more meta-
physical than otherwise
from this angle

also there is something on the floor in the foreground
which might be a crumpled bag or a few dead
sweatshirts or
i don't know but the pity is
that the lecturer was so boring
i got all lulled up and forgot to go look at the book
when the lecture was over

and getting back to you
you will never be sweet
i realize now that whether things go well or ill
there's no changing your weather
so i still feel strange

in the dream i'm not sure i purchased any of those houses
but i did kiss those realtors in the face of the world's problems
and i'm sure you understand why i'm feeling very guilty

# THE DIFFERENCE BETWEEN 166 & 165

you have forgotten the street names and numbers
of all the places where we used to sleep
and wake and drowse and sleep again

this is not the way the story was written
with a bouquet of orange roses in a cobalt blue vase
languishing on the table next to two electric candles

this is not the way subtraction is accomplished
the sudden rending of one number from another
without serious cause, without compassionate warning

without a simple reply to a simple question
but this is the way the world works and when
you and i approach it this is the answer we receive:

silk millinery flowers. artificial limbs. raveled rigging ripped
from the flanks of damaged ferries that try to travel
between one consciousness and the next
on the black uncharted waters

# THIS PROCEDURE IS NOT DANGEROUS, ALTHOUGH YOU WILL FEEL SOME PAIN

I walk up to you and insert my key. I open the mahogany door to the white corridor where a single chain hangs from the ceiling: no one knows why. The corridor is unlit, but its whiteness suffices. I walk into you. You scream. Literally you say hello politely, but I know you scream. The chain is not attached to any light. I pull it. You kiss me. I pull it again. You scream. This time it is real and the noise echoes in orange waves along your ribs and backbone. I stand there in my kind dress. I do not believe I am lost. I believe all the screaming will guide me. I hold up my key in the whiteness of the corridor and am struck by how it is shaped like you. I hold out my hand and am burned by the scream, but still I do not go back.

# STOP EQUATING LOVE WITH LOSS

the seventeen monks at the candystore are not lost or loved
except by each other

they remember the barkcloth drapes of their childhoods and their mothers
stretching to hang them

they remember silences in the rain buckets and squirrel hills like toques
on balding heads before the day's chatter

before the day's chatter could begin they smooth themselves as if they were
covered in silky fur, that's how smooth they are

the twelve no seventeen monks took themselves to tea
in the therapy room and sat for once in chairs

no more sprinkling the blessed water on chanting hordes no more
singing to the singing brass bowls or single blossoms

here the seventeen no twenty monks must lord it over
their best-hidden dreams

they are wandering around in a sparsely-treed forest like the one
in that low-budget stupid movie

with the crosses in the trees thinking it's supposed to be scary
but it's not

they were not blind but they were acting that way and they were all
in low voices, in unison, intoning

"WE ..... ARE ..... LOST"
with great pauses between the words and then one young monk screamed

"RSVP your sleepwalker!" and all the bells broke loose
from interior cymbals and rang through the therapy room like a breeze

it is true then that some of them died, but some lived on
and to this very day the others speak of the dead with caution

# HIGH SCHOOL

who's miss string in love with?

jeanemarie's stiffly ironed shirt
miss tooth always laughing
sister margretina and her famous loaf of bears

please do not hurt me oh i am absurd

"parce que nous ne pouvons pas dormir"
repeated through the meager falling night
like a wildflower

# WE ARE GETTING ALL UPSET OVER NOTHING

Living alone you get warped and believe
everything. There is no more
contemporary life, just as there was
no philosopher's stone and nowhere
in the library to look it up. Go slowly
or you will get lost. Construct
the afternoon like this: hunger,
a bruised shin, the grey skirts of clouds
rising over Building A. I want to leave
love out of this, but now
it's in. She sits on a rock wall, reads,
and plans that he'll come by. The conversation
goes like this: nod, smile, touch, laugh,
take off glasses. He moves on, obliged
by a previous happiness. Living alone
you overhear everything. Leave out
birds, no automotive sounds. In the clear
silence she enters Building R; as she goes
downstairs he turns off the lights: photo-
sensitivity. He turns them on.
He is cluttered with sadness, obligations
to contemporary pals. She feels
the scar on his back, the happiness
that cannot be undone. The whole construction
falls, the string of enchantments
something to tie on the tap
to soften the dripping. Otherwise
it drives her mad.

# DUSK

1.
i am walking along beacon street and it is slightly raining and i have been talking to people about things they should be knowing and i have been remembering that these things i already know about should be helping me too

and i am lying in bed with the grey-lavender covers pulled up and the softness of egyptian cotton and i am amazed at my weakness and at my abstraction and at my transitory nature

next to me you are sleeping
at last sleeping
a long sleep you need you have trouble
when you sleep you are gone i am gone we are gone

and i am thinking of you and your secrets and my secrets and his secrets and even hers

and i am sorry

and there are lights on the side of the building that remind me of midnight in the back yard in ramsey new jersey as we waited for a sighting of the color red of mars

bats

northern lights around edges

lamps in scarce windows

whole town sleeping like you

what more would we have learned if we'd had a telescope that evening
what more about father

what more about mother
what more about the red dog in her warm house sleeping
and the planet all red in its sky

2.
i have heard from someone recently about 'deep disappointment'
i am she
i have been speaking about it
i have been strange

i imagine a movie in which person 1 says person 2 will probably
            do / give / say
x in my direction
i do not know how person 1 is dressed or if it is a she
i do not know how to talk to her

what i (person 2) want to say to her is 'expect nothing'
after all these years if (s)he is expecting something or expecting something specific
(s)he will experience
'deep disappointment'

3.
it is curious to me how the children are young
they are not blake's children
or even yours
they resent blake's old clothes
i resent when they speak of their mothers
who are older than me but know more
i resent not knowing more now
not no-ing

4.
i could play this song for you on the harmonium but it is *pusillanimous*
we define the word differently
we are coasting on different memories of the word

i think i will send you a package

in this package will be my baby words my bonnet
no that's not right
in this package will be my shroud and my last will and testament

i leave you
all

5.
now it will be nine years
please measure change
please fill donation bucket with expectations
expect it to be emptied

do not speak of 'deep disappointment' unless you are planting it in the garden next to the hollow piece of log where the thrushes ramble

do not ramble

do not ask me so many questions because unlike the mothers of the children who are older than me i have no information

or i have little information

or i have no information i want to 'share' with you

at this time

6.
he held some kind of light show in the library
his wife said *he did not lose face*
a phrase i find peculiar and revealing

7.
they identify meanness as a sympton of envy
the word is *ardent*
and we struggle to define it
are you zealous fervid earnest
impassioned
have you said your five hail marys
do you confess my sins

i believe you are truly sorry

penitent remorseful contrite apologetic
possibly relevant

and that sores on the soul can be healed

# SNOW-WET FIELD, NOVEMBER

In a way one is chosen by llamas—a particular way. One and two coming up to you in a field from far away, picking their way along the snow-caused stream, taking their time, all of us have time, one of them rubbing his neck against the fence, slowly, up and down, slowly, what pleasure, one bowing her head to graze the flowers, yellow, the small flowers, and sometimes whitish green, then one by one coming right up to you, one and two, not quite touching but you can feel their eyelash breeze. Do not doubt us they say and the choosing is definite though the plot sometimes unclear, I might say most times unclear, but the choosing so often a brilliant warm light, clear and so startling, sudden water on the eyes. In the nearby barn waits the sheep who was once a girl, the sheep who is writing her memoirs, and the goat Snow White with magnificent brow, the goat who chose her name. Sun blankets the snow-cold field and the llamas have asked you for pictures, give us art they say, let everyone decorate everything, the chickens do, see the hens pushing out their skirts in the sawdust, see the proud roosters sketching lines in the shale. We need colors out here! The llamas' backs are broad, broad as your armspan, broad the sheep's shoulders, the goat's broad brow. Heaven leans low. Mud begins in the meadow. Someone serves lunch in the long red house, someone hums to a picture of silence. Pull back the latch, pull back the door, the goat's ripped your coat, the grey pony grumbles. The barn's full of sparrows, the ducks waltz in line. And the great shining white horse she trembles.

# FIREFLIES

the grapevines begin to flower in ways we have not expected

microscopic dust insects in books
those little red spiders

a cry in the night
sharp
and high
like an otter who's dropped his clam

the optician who talked about reincarnation
maybe you'll come back with better eyesight he said

remember to check when you close the garage
that there are no birds inside

# A PTARMIGAN

These two—they have such a pale understanding
of each other—not pale in a washed-out way but pale
as in understated, fine, subtle,
like a pale wine-stain that becomes part of the fabric's design
and would be missed if removed. And here they are,
two people on a very small island (the size, let's say,
of a 1950's convertible), in the dark, in the fog,
with the silken waters lapping
all around, and they are not afraid
exactly, just weary. They've brought with them, as always,
flashlights; one even has a lantern. They have
jackets, waterproof ones, and they have
conversation of an interesting type and they have bright,
bright eyes
in the darkness. They do not touch, for they do not
know each other well, but you can tell they will touch
at some undesignated future point, or would touch
if circumstances demanded it—would touch in a minute—
to save themselves, say, if the water rose too high,
or to huddle together if the wind became too fierce,
or the rain. Or they would touch if the conversation,
now at another interesting juncture—clever, you might say,
although never sarcastic—turned to reveal that one of them
suffered pain. What are they saying? In the cool drift
of the water and the night, delicate words can be heard
on the brine-scented air. One mentions a book, the other pretends
to have read it, but knows enough about it in fact
to be able to ask a fair question. This goes on for some time
and they are growing somewhat cold
and wearier, and although they do not like to admit it,
a little afraid. A ptarmigan dips down through the fog
to look at them, yet they do not kiss. The expressions
on their faces are kind, if puzzled, if bemused. What they do
not know is that the land is just nearby

beyond where the fog drops off and their line of vision
dissolves.  They can hear the frogs on shore
beguiling their mates in deep voices,
yet their weariness stops them from believing
they could stretch out their four hands and touch them.

*(for Mulder and Scully)*

She kept his dream between two flat covers, the cardboard extending
down the right, through the center, and over the left of
the dream, buckling
somehow, if dreams do that, where the softest interior
bled, inconveniently, for the crimson was such
a bother to her, in keeping the hidden dream

white. The hard mark of his beauty left
a transit, a light within light within
light, or was it a touch or something overheard, the
"belated eloquence of the inarticulate" flashing on a night
when all the things she carried around were bound
by a gravity pulled to a working idea
in the room between the word and the quest for the word,
that's where

she had hidden him. Here's his head, somewhat
lonelier now, but finally as close
as ever. In riding it up and down, between blue curtains
and into
red nights, she'd given, she felt, the last wrong excuse
to his wrists. They "fell in" so,
like birds; the wrists *fell in*, as if birds falling
were terribly thin and drawn to the exit of light
by air, air spinning, her body then drawn in silk, a long,
a dove-
grey silk of leaves, a wristlet of smoke, a rose-white rose
and a jewel confounding them all

in her eye. She told him
"what she did all day." She had
the perfect foreignness with him, all white,
the way a mountain desert can contain
itself and the perfection of the strange.

# THREAT

You are dangerous to me
because of your beauty
not really dangerous
no real beauty
neither the delicacy of flowers
nor the immensity of landscapes
not even the smoothness of marble
but the length of your nose
the tapping of your foot
the secrecy of your sins
of these I am afraid.

Yes, I would bring you a bowl of hot soup
containing white muddy boots
and blue china grasshoppers
and looking into its steam you would see
the repetition of your terrors
the finale of your creaseless trousers
not to forget your invisible boutonniere.

I do not know why I am angry
when I have only just met you
I hear you speak
like an instant cloud
that brightens everything by its darkness

# BELIEF SYSTEMS

I didn't want to read
anything after that, I didn't
want to write or eat or speak
to anyone about it, it was too
bleak, too beautiful, too like a
gene without DNA, a sparkle
of a fleck of an atom
of the moon, the moon of a planet
not yet discovered, I wished
for a mystery like that to detail
my life, to keep the beans
boiling somewhere off to the left,
where electricity was explained to me
for the thousandth time, but this time
it worked, both the lamps
and the candles, this time I breathed
far less than the machines
could calculate, I mystified
the doctors, who still believed
I would find you in the dark, that you
would still be shining for me after all
these years, although to me it had never
mattered
that you had no eyes, it mattered
to others, they could not
forgive you, they took your phone calls
and put them in a drawer, they believed
you had some money
that they might inherit some day,
but they didn't even care. Any more. After
a while. Whenever
you say. I "bled out on the table" the doctor
said twice, I
was dead, I was

in heaven, I crunched
a celestial cookie, gladly, even while
the plumber was still there in the house, repairing
a noxious leak and breaking
all the wine glasses. Dead and buried,
that's me, forgotten and re-
remembered. I've gone out
"over the transom." Nice
that you called.

# THE CORGIS OF QUEEN ELIZABETH

on wednesday september 10th 2003 i was visiting my friend larry
who is chronically ill
larry knows everything about the corgis
and queen elizabeth
who now has five or six corgis
who mill about her feet and the feet of her dressmakers
and all the kings and queens before elizabeth
and he knows what the corgis have for breakfast
and he knows that they get fresh vegetables not raw
and they get turkey
in little silver bowls
cut up in little cubes not slices
and queen elizabeth serves them their meals herself
she had a favorite corgi named daisy
whom she buried somewhere on the palace grounds
with a little corgi funeral
and i do not mean to make fun of that
because i am happy she loved her corgi
but let's be clear it does not always mean
that a person who loves a different kind of creature
is totally good
as i understand hitler loved canaries
and not to compare her to hitler
but queen elizabeth also indulges in hunting
and we all know about those presidential dogs

while larry is talking i'm thinking this is very fascinating
but i'm also watching the digital clock
over his shoulder
which displays hours minutes weather wind velocity
and alerts you whenever the airport closes in boston
if there are disasters of any kind
this is a very special clock
that he bought with part of the money that he received

from his suit against the massachusetts bay transit authority
occasioned by a trolley driver closing the door of the trolley
on his already painful foot
as part of his affliction is a dreadful neuropathy
to which he rarely refers
although that trolley incident really pissed him off
because the driver could have easily seen his crutches

he tells me the corgis have their own bedroom
next to the bedroom of queen elizabeth and prince philip
yes the queen does sleep with the prince even now
except on the nights when he's out very late
and comes home after she has retired
when politely he goes and sleeps on a special princely bed
right in his dressing room
the corgis however always sleep in their own room
just next to the queen's own queenly bedroom
and recently when a man
was somehow able to break into the palace
and walk boldly into the queen's suite of rooms
finding the queen cloaked and crowned in terrycloth
as she had just taken her queenly evening bath
and was carrying her gin tray and a big yellow towel
the queen was most relieved that the corgis were not able
to get out of their bedroom
because she feared that they would have used
their little diamond-sharp teeth
to shred the silly man like turkey
so loyal and so fierce (but so sweet) are those corgis

and while larry is telling me about the queen and the corgis
and throwing in a lot of extra information about prince charles
and camilla and how camilla and her father
actually have suites of rooms in one of the royal buildings
where diana's sons now live
(i cannot understand how this can be true
but larry swears it is)

in any case all this amazing information pours out of larry
in a way that i never would have believed possible
since he is normally a rather circumspect fellow
and while i'm watching the airport clock
over his right shoulder
i'm watching over his left shoulder
his tiny television
which for some unknown reason he has set to show captions
for the hard of hearing
they are showing newly released tapes from al qaeda
showing pictures of osama bin laden
or someone made up to look like osama bin laden
walking up and down the hillsides
somewhere
looking a lot like a shepherd

from the old testament
and underneath the captions are reading
"is it osama?
is it not osama?"
there is an investigation to try to find out
whether the tape is real or a hoax
and whether the soundtrack (or what shows on larry's tv
as italicized captions) was added to the tape after the video
was shot and i'm thinking
what difference does that make
it doesn't mean that it isn't really osama
or even that it isn't really
a shepherd from the old testament

and perhaps it's all happening in cleveland or barcelona or honolulu
and not in afghanistan or iraq or hollywood
or any of the places we're always being conditioned to think
are the only places anything of significance ever happens
when really everything is happening right here
right here with the corgis and queen elizabeth and larry
and the trolley driver and the lawyer who handled larry's case

and the democratic presidential candidates
and the people who are sitting out on their stoops
just the way people did fifty years ago
on washington street in jamaica plain
but it's right here and not twenty years ago or five years from now and

everything's happening right here
right here where you hear or read this and make up your mind about it
right here and right now and not anywhere else forever

# BAD LADYBUG DAYS

Everything started out okay and C said he was sleepy and I had a waking dream. And I read about the woman who didn't like being in the house with her husband all the time, and it turned out she had a good reason: the anger hours. Then I found what I thought was a ladybug larva turning into a ladybug on a hairbrush in the bathroom, but when I carried it outside to set it free, I realized it was already dead and had already turned into a little desiccated skeleton. Which made me remember the other day when I was in the ladies' room at that college and I saw a little ladybug on the floor and decided to take her and her brightness outside with me, and I got her to walk onto my hand and then onto a little piece of paper, and on that I carried her outside, but it was a windy rainy day, very windy, and suddenly before I could find a leaf or anything to put her down on, a gust of wind came along and blew her off the little piece of paper and onto a parking meter. She wasn't moving. And when I put my finger down next to her another gust of wind came along and blew her to the ground, where she landed on her back. I turned her over but I'm pretty sure she was dead then, but of course you never know—sometimes they're just playing dead, so that is what I hoped. But it's too bad really that two days this week I tried to save ladybugs and couldn't.

# THINGS IN DRAWERS

it was a very realistic fight scene, a paralyzing dream where
the players looked for something lost
with a clear flashlight (inside you could see all the parts
the batteries the switch etc.)
and then stopped to discuss the cultural dilemma
that 99% of audiences leave the theater before the credits run

there are several myths surrounding my birth

i was not born in a blizzard
but three days later

i was not born in an orphanage
but in a part of the hospital that had once been an orphanage

i regret these misconceptions
which i myself at times have fostered

# STONETTE

oh god i have got to stop purchasing anthills!
stonette you are urging me in the wrong direction, alas.
why have i listened to you again you are clearly mistaken.
you encourage me to speak my inmost soul at the drop of a petal
and yet you do not appear in time
to sweep the petals up.

stonette, you beleaguer me i cannot sweetly breathe.
my opinion about her mother stands as fact
you cannot know. why did you sleep with her could you not
smell the future?

oh stonette i had such fun with you in the greenhouse can we not
go there again?

i got up early on my birthday it was
colder than hell the stars were ice-pick holes
in an indigo mirror the moon
three-quarters gone. i sat lopsided
over the barn my husband still asleep and restless dreams
around and through the troubles
this life has brought us. stonette

this is a good day to start the right time
to begin to say
no more. he has moved away hasn't he hasn't he?
he never loved your slow music
just his dental-office jazz.

stonette you don't know how we miss you come home.
oh there are no babies here to scream or shit.

here it is shadowless.

# MORE TO SAY

Why do I know it comes from the Nile: your mysterious
kindness? A magnificent place
to visit, but there's more to say. And the sweet
quiet space
between the rain and the ground, the stillness like the space
between bouts of illness
when the patient seems to sleep
and the flowers seem to fly
from their vases
and circle the mourners' heads
and dip down here and there and christen them
with the relief of hopelessness
and the colors ivory and zie-blau, sea-blue. Is it
Egyptian then? And a river? There's more
to say. When what's said
sounds foolish
there's more to say. Whether what's said
is thunderclap or mouse-voice
there's more to say. If the back of the tongue
is grey, if the heart
flickers, if the blackbird turns
redbird and sings
opera
there's more to say. There's more
under the desk blotter, more
inside the hatband, more sewn into
the hem of my skirt, more in the honey-yellow, more
in your lavender whiskers, more in the morning,
more in the evening mourners, more
forever. Whether we sit on the riverbank,
swoon on the riverbed, drink
up the river's bend, there's always
more to say. Whether it rains on our fingers or not,
whether we entwine them or not,

want to entwine them
fear to entwine them,
in dreams entwine them
there's still more to say. Whether you give me
that look of the Nile or not, there'll be more
to say. If you make me wait
forever
for the myth of the right moment,
for the sighting of six zebras (white on white),
for this room to be tiled in zie-blau,
there will still
be more to say. Your unthinkable
kindness, your Egyptian satchel
of rivers, your
hatband burial outfit, your goings
without comings: you call them all
the last word, but you see
that is impossible. In the beginning
was a word. In the beginning a word
opened. A word
opened and a word took power
and a word was spoken
and spoken
and spoken. Nothing
can stop it. No one
can *not* say it. You may sew up your mouth
with a fork and a knife
(as you have
done). You may sew up your eyes of Nile
with crocodile (as you have
done). You may tell me you do not believe
there's anything left
to talk about. You may gaze down properly
into the grave, but it won't
end there: the stones are speaking.
You can't ignore them. There is no
last word: the stones

are speaking. This country
goes on forever: the stones are speaking.
They will say what you cannot say if you ask them.
You will say what they cannot say if they ask you and I
will be listening. Listen:
there is more
than what the stones say
and more
than what the rivers say
and more than even the words themselves say so please
don't worry about what you didn't say: you said it.
The country of you and you, the country
of me and me: you said it, it's
endless; it is not
Egypt, and there's still more to say.
You can now stop
forever
shielding your eyes,
you can stop now forever
pretending you see the borders.
When you do speak, speak slowly, and observe how each line
coils out into the future
as if to lasso
the uncreated.

# A BLOCKBUSTER THRILLER OF MELODY AND DESIRE

b sings for louise bourgeois

i am not there—this is hearsay
inadmissible in court

the room is dark and there are fading tulips
in a vase on the piano
b is singing

the room is quiet because everyone is surprised

not louise

not b

not b's wife

not the piano

nor anyone he tells later

b is singing and his nervousness he says
makes his voice more vibrant

he opens his mouth
his hands sleep on his knees
then flutter

b's drawings lie on a hardwood drafting table near the window

gulls hesitate
then fall

when he sings the corners of the drawings lift up

he wears his green shirt
which is soft as spring water

# SLOWER LEAPER

The entire coastline has been converted into some kind of theme park—not an offensive one, but one that more closely, we seem to feel, parallels life. And as if on a conveyor belt we glide out along a long boardwalk that stretches out into the sea and suddenly the boardwalk ends and there is a moving platform, about five feet square and painted white; it is separated from the piece of boardwalk on which we stand—the three of us—and it moves and sways back and forth in front of us and we know that we must leap onto it as it passes us—and it does this in quick moments only, so that there is a great chance of missing it, of falling roughly into the sea below, or even of falling and hitting the base of the platform, which is made of steel and dangerous. You and she don't even think: you leap; of course you make it. I am left deliberating on the other side, and while I know I can make it if I try, I am immersed in a sense of loss of the two of you—two of you who have once and for all abandoned the slower leaper.

# PRUSSIAN BLUE

there are suicides and there are suicides
some done in red
some blue

i believe yours is blue
or would be
not that you'd ever do it

but i read that john polidori (author of *the vampyre* with a "y"
late 18th century)
used prussic acid
which is actually related somehow chemically
to the color prussian blue

and i thought of you

around the same era
mary woolstonecraft
tried to drown herself in the thames but was kept afloat
by her billowing skirts

which is not how i would do it
having the benefit of her experience

not that i would do anything like that of course

i think there are no yellow suicides
impossible to do yourself in
in yellow
unless maybe you're approaching that dandelion color on a rainy day
i can't be sure

i am certain you're still alive
although i know you died last wednesday

or did you die when i said no on tuesday
or yes on monday

you can't fool me

you always do

there's suicide all over the hotel soap
suicide in the soup tureen
suicide hankies for teacup coverlets
with buttons sewn on the corners as weights
to keep the flies out of your tea

suicide wallets full of suicide money
suicide triplets (all die the same day)
national triplet suicide day in fact
celebrated widely
suicide finger-foods
for that pre-death picnic feast

when mary woolstonecraft actually did die
it was never suicide
she died after giving birth to her daughter
and suffered such unconventional complications
that puppies were brought to suckle her bursting breasts
sadly to no avail

i hope she loved puppies

she dreamed then of the thames
her plaid skirts filling up with fishes
swimming puppies
swimming babies
small wet feet

and golems you know only die
if the "e" is erased from their foreheads

so the life-word forms death in their language

their clay bodies melt like candles
their golem brains gutter
and sputter
and die

it's a wonderful story
an anti-suicide

the story i will tell you if you ask
for i am told you're bound to ask some day
and i must be prepared

i will set out my weapons
my koolaid colored poisons
my silken blue pajamas
my eraser and my eye

you will kindly allow me to watch you
to ascertain you do not die

# THE BOOK OF SLEEPERINA

**1.**
**s_l_e_e_p_e_r_i_n_a**

my name is sleeperina and you will find no information to support that
claim

i have no namesake

the speed of connection approaches the end of the world

when sleeperina concocts her breakfast all states of the world collapse in
spain

my name is sleeperina

i have felt no instinct to reproduce

i have seen a bad movie in which you appeared as bane

what is to say that profile is any realer than the standing

he is bugjuice

looks like the funny papers

but he loves us

**2.**
**sleeperina describes her bed**

when i drove down to the lower level of the parking garage there was an abandoned portrait of jack kennedy and a used computer. later i told miss l. about that. i sent m. some salve for his head but it turned out to smell like cat piss. inside the pine tree the forest was tall. some confusion about spelling. my bed has a vowel in it. last night everyone expected everything and i have only this bed and my sleeping to offer. will he think me sexy. will the goshawk finish the skeleton in time. we've decided the tiny skull must be from a woodchuck. we give it a place of honor in our house.

**3.**
**brief family history of sleeperina**

if there were *bad* germans then we are ashamed

one was a jeweler

in new jersey all sizes of fingers

george washington the name i remember for grandpa

whom i never met

a family concerned with grammars

heart problems no cancers just attics

attics that smelled like hair

mrs. e. who sat on a canary

greatgrandma-mah with her lifelong uncut braid

white candles and altars the infant of prague

once thinking it's called 'the infamous frog'

brother like a beetroot

tiny handles

**4.**
**spoiled in love**

so it was new year's eve and i thought i had to see you. i drove the icy highway until i could pretend i slid off the road. pretended to be terrified. drove back home and called you. you understood.

it was our first real date and i thought we had to have it. i spent a long time in the bathroom deciphering you. maybe four years give or take. when i came out you were watching television and snacking. i .

i confessed to being sleeperina.

we said goodbye.

**5.**
**sleeperina discourses on pornography**

she was not certain there even was any

she saw it around the corner

it was not william burroughs it was not playboy

it was not exactly wrong
no not even wrong

it's just that it was her heart and her heartbeat and her woman
and her valentine
he ignored

**6.**
**today sleeperina began to crack the shell**

and crawled out wet into the world all shaky

she would not have time for any nonsense

she again attempted to describe her bed like this

a blue oval

an oval bluebird

she attempted to say love

to turn *she* finally to *i*

proudly sleeperina forgave the masses

she stood on the dome of elegiac chessboard and sang

**7.**
**text without music of sleeperina's song**

i'm a little sass-mouth
thin and stout
here is my ego
here is my pout

**8.**
**translation of #7 (sleeperina's song)**

no matter what i say to you
i do not hear your real answer

no matter how you cry to me
i have not seen your real tears

no matter how you touch me
i know there's a handkerchief between us

if i remove the handkerchief

well if i do...

**9.**
**in all belief a tincture of stone**

i am all unaware of your panels of flight

if i knew how to please you
i would not try
the way i do now

sleeperina looks at herself in the mirror
and sees sleeperina defining her bed again
she never gets tired

earlier in the world there were no details

it was a fine vague time
no one wanted the whole story
if there was a bird you just said it was a bird not a goshawk
if there was a tree it was a tree not a slippery elm

if your secrets left tracks in the snow
if your secrets...

**10.**
**epilogue: pretend (fake) sonnet for the young sleeperina**

your secrets leave tracks in the snow

secret tracks that's why no one can see them

i imagined i would tell you about an owl
i imagined you'd understand that owl and wash it

fourteen lines in every sonnet but this one
this is a section not a stanza
i have not combed my hair all day

i backed into his car when i drove out the driveway
a white car that looked just like a snowbank

i still think it must have been a snowbank
a snowbank turned into a car

the way memories crowd must mean something
when sleeperina was a child she had a recurring dream
a faraway house surrounded by a wall
there were pastel colors the trees were pale
the lawn was mint green and it was not kelly
the wall was piled with large round stones

sleeperina was standing on the outside looking in

is the moon turned left or right
in this vision
left or right?

# THE TREES

You can't explain everything. You can't even begin to explain everything. As soon as you say a word you need to explain it. As soon as you write a word it needs explaining. What does word mean what does explain mean what does what mean. What. And if you stop for a minute you are doomed. If you stop to remember taking that photograph in the basement when you were ill you are doomed. If you stop to remember what you stopped to remember you're doomed. If you stop to examine the photograph or even the word photograph forget it. You just can't do it. You've got to keep going. There's not enough time and there aren't enough words and there's too much going on in the trees.

# LITTLE MATCHES

there's an awful lot of hanging around listening
a huge bruise
a private waiting room
a quiet air conditioner
a kind joke
a quiet hand
i can't help it i'm falling up the mountain
(but maybe not quite as quietly as before)

a hand behind the potted plant now
(someone listening)
a ring on the wrong finger
quotation marks versus parentheses
we said they could pick the snapdragons while we were gone

i don't know if sol lewitt said murals are weightless
or if i wrote that on a card while looking at a painting

i didn't say the painting was his

i honestly can't remember

but rothko i believe actually said
*unite the object and its meaning*

i saw that in the connecticut museum
where c took a series of pictures of me looking at pictures
that turned out funny—me looking suspicious
as if i were casing the joint to make off with the paintings

and in a way i suppose i was

i would give them to you

it made me remember my great grandmother's hair and altars
she who (reputedly) had never cut her hair
she who worshipped (devoutly)
in front of the infant of prague
who was dressed in real clothes

a fine plaster statue with red velvet cape and beaded white garments
one tiny hand raised as if the fingers would burst into flame

austria
in the spring of her childhood
before many wars
the infant of salzburg

in age she became paper-faced
as i am doing
in age she became tiny
as i may yet do

DID YOU HEAR THE GREAT THUNDER WHILE WE WERE SLEEPING?

i read my affirmations
from a green slip of paper in my wallet
*it is safe to be vulnerable* the paper says
which i affirm while doubting its truth

i read someone is assigning the ablative absolute
preposterously

you could be more sensitive

magpies on the split-rail fence
at the corner of your sister's city
not sister-city (dushanbe, japan) who gave you a teahouse
we were too hurried to visit

we bought ripe cherries

and held the pits in our cold white fingers
before realizing we could throw them on the ground

YOU CAN NEVER REMOVE ALL DANGER

it is within you always
it always safely shines

# SELF ENVELOPE

i am cutting the pages of joe brainard's *i remember*
because this last copy came with some of the pages still folded at the top
and i wondered if i should cut them
or just peek inside and read them
i wondered then i opted for the easier way out

in colorado i saw some stationery in the museum store that i wanted
but it was too expensive and i realized i could make it myself
it was the kind where you fold over the sheet to make a self envelope
then you seal the little flap and it's all compact and clever

then in massachusetts again in a junk store i came upon some foreign
  stationery
of the very same style
with funny phrases printed on it in english
like *are you feel better?* and *fruits shooting*
whatever in the world that means
and some were pink and some aquamarine and some were shades of brown
and some said *treasures of memory*

and all these priceless little stationery packages were two for a dollar
i bought six and had my laugh at the overpriced museum store

i sent some to my brother
and will send some to some others

it's appalling how tired i'm feeling today
but i worked hard yesterday and i guess that's the price you pay
for not being any spring chicken

i read that the new *school of philosophic revenge*
had something to do with courage
but i swear i can't really understand what that means

# COLLAGE = TO GLUE

it is the color of the chicory flower i would like that
along with the color of the edges of the fading phlox
some white or lime green to go with it

geographically i am weak

w says she'd like to make the handyman her "permanent friend"

b sends a lovely little piece about some joe brainard confusions
and a coffin in the living room
in which he mentions me and my brother and some other people i don't
    know

i called miss j but she hasn't called me back

it's the chicory color i want most of all
the particular blue of that flower
considered a weed
or a wildflower by the generous minded
and with it the color of the edges of the fading phlox
a little lime green or white on the side
would do for now

i'd probably tell you everything if i thought you could hear me

in the night in the dream in the night dream i'm falling
through layers and layers of a wide weird bed
you wake me and ask about nightmares
my right arm sore from reaching above my head

i thought i could reach the light but it was not handy
i thought i could get to that color
i thought i could name it

i thought he was "good with languages"
but i was mistaken

some delicate detail has faded
off my brand-new filigree ring

# WHITE PEANUTS

Boiled in brine. This makes me remember Canada. Five or so of us stood in the parking-lot of a bar outside Vancouver and T said "Are you all right?" and he had that look on his face that people get when they say that really meaning "I know you're not all right because of something I've done but I'm going to try to turn it back on you and make you believe you're acting strangely so that you'll get confused and I'll feel better." I've heard it before. But he had this cellophane bag of white peanuts that were boiled in brine and I'd never seen anything like it. I asked him about it. "Local specialties," he said, still looking at me funny. I'd ignored his question. I'd asked one of my own. These things were not permitted. He put on his strange golfing cap and looked back at me once like an owl and got into his car.

# COELACANTH

This is not leap year. I have forgotten the list I was given in the dream—truths about myself—in the Chinese knickknack boutique. There were at least ten or eleven of them, and the first had to do with that conversation with N about L, where N asked me why nobody could bear to be around L "any more," including me. But I had never been able to bear him. And also in the dream the Orange Line trains, leaving as they used to from an above-ground station, and me walking through the puddles to them on platform shoes, not getting my feet wet. The pleasant warm puddles. And the whole good feeling of the dream, perhaps because I picked up the old understanding from G, and from R too, with his terrible dead flapping feet. G was always so tall? A sea-city dream? A tray of handmade earrings. Then at work one day I used the word "Muriel," deliberately, in place of a more boring word, and everyone laughed. Must have been the thin handwriting and the lungfish in the natural history museum. Might have been the lionfish, though, or the coelacanth. Those lacy dark skeletons; one of them might be mine. Three hundred and eighty years old I think it said. Or something higher.

# SHOPPING

I am with a blonde woman picking out earrings when I realize she has bad taste. Not in earrings necessarily but she is holding a copy of a book by a famous but worthless novelist who has trashed a book I love. I don't know this blonde woman, or even if she is blonde. She looks suspiciously at me. We leave the jewelry counter and go for a cup of coffee; while she is standing on line I realize I've lost my shopping bag. It contained some clothes I was taking away for the weekend. I go back to the hotel where I'd been staying, only to find they were already renting my room, with my stuff still in it. Some of it had been thrown away, but there was a polite young man there who seemed to understand the situation and was willing to let me poke around. I found a belt of mine and a shoe in the closet. At least I thought it was my shoe, but then realized it was his. The belt was mine. The room was no longer mine. The shopping bag was lost. But I had also lost track of the blonde woman and I was happy.

# DURING THE MOZART STRING QUARTET IN D

we have very good seats up front off to the side
in the high-ceilinged hall on an april afternoon a sunday
and i am suddenly obsessed with the shoes of the young woman violinist
the violinist from riga latvia
who began playing violin at age five
and relocated at age twenty-one
to dallas texas
and is now in boston massachusetts
playing afternoon mozart
inside a contemporary chapel
where the names of the donors are etched on little bronze strips
set discreetly into concrete-stippled walls

i am obsessed with her nice black shoes
because although they are similar i am convinced they are not a pair
and she must have gotten up in a hurry from a very deep nap
and slipped her feet hurriedly into her shoes
perhaps in a murky walk-in latvian-texan closet
not realizing she was wearing two different black pumps
similar but from different pairs

her biography (on pink photocopy paper) informs us
she has played with both itzhak perlman
and linda ronstadt
i find this fascinating
i imagine her extraordinary classical violin life
full of fragrant bouquets and many black outfits
that fit her classical form almost right
and which she throws around carelessly until there are piles of black clothes
        everywhere
then off she dashes to the cleaners
depositing a rose-sacheted pile on the counter

and receiving a smile from one of her many fans

she has good legs and favors high-heeled shoes
stylish but not trendy
more classical than contemporary you might say
and yet she has trouble finding just the right fit
and therefore has quite a few pairs
it's especially difficult to find the right height of heel
because sitting down playing the violin she moves her legs around a lot
sometimes resting one toe on the edge of the music stand
sometimes not

today she has made a little error
which i am pleased to discover
i feel intimately related to her in some way as if we are girlfriends
and over the phone she might say to me "you know
it was so terribly embarrassing
today at the concert i wore two different shoes
i wonder if anyone noticed"

i am not just the girlfriend but the person who noticed
i slip a pen out of my purse
and write on the edge of the program "woman—
different shoes?"
and nudge my husband

he looks at the paper
he looks at the shoes

he looks at me and shakes his head
no
and makes little motions with his hands
signifying the shoes are at different angles
in his opinion
i am experiencing an optical illusion
in his opinion
something tells me i already knew this before i asked

i look again at the shoes
the two different shoes
i blink my eyes
hoping my vision will clear
i decide to wait
for the woman to change the position of her feet
then she does and

the shoes are obviously different

one is a suave sort of shoe
very streamlined and thin
one is more clunky
less revealing
but probably more comfortable
this sturdy shoe is on her left foot
the one she most often
props against the music stand
things begin to make more sense

i nudge my husband
whisper illegally during the solo
"the shoes" i whisper
"the shoes" i mouth silently
so he looks again
intently
shakes his head
no
and goes back to the music

but i cannot go back
for a long time
finally i force myself
back into the allegretto
complicated as it is
it comforts me in this world

where shoes play perplexing games with me

but eventually i look at her feet again
expecting the shoes to have come to their senses
and match each other
but alas
they do not

and the concert ends
to rousing applause
and the woman violinist leaves her seat
and stands with her three colleagues
to receive our acclaim

there she stands in front of us
in plain plain sight

*her shoes are the same*
*identical*
*exactly alike*
*twins each to the other*
*different only in left and right*

my husband says
"the angle"
and continues his applauding
he is not in the least concerned
with the depth of my confusion

i say "i see that now"
and am astonished

i say "i see that now"
and gaze down at my feet

# JUST ONE THING

It occurs to me that the problem is that I keep thinking that I'll be able to fix something so that it will stay fixed—not change. For example if I cut my nails correctly I won't have to do it again, or if I get the garden to look just perfectly the way I want it nothing will grow or change or get ruined by hail or slugs—or if I could just for once just once get you to see how imperfectly I have loved you, that would explain everything for all time for both of us. This foolishness is a huge thing—a Buddhist I think would advise me about it. If I could find the right Buddhist that Buddhist would advise me and then everything would be all right forever and not change.

# TRAPUNTO

**1.**

in a repressed society there will be a lot of silence because silence is contagious and if you're not allowed to say certain things eventually you won't want to say others either and there won't be a lot of good things said
g said
"i really like potatoes" or
"of course you like potatoes"
it was a joke between us

then he slipped in "i'm never going
to get well"

and i remembered j had said something like that to me years ago
as he served the tea
sweet tea in big glass mugs

in *trapunto* the design is outlined with two or more rows of running stitches
and then padded from the underside to achieve a raised effect

here's what i remember of his story

he was a genius child
he picked up broken pieces of glass and fashioned them into trees
ghosts followed him around with baskets to pick up genius words
he might let fall
somebody loved him
but ignorantly

was it a dream i had NO
not a dream
trapunto with his head in his hands a headache
the headache a trapeze on which he walked unsteadily falling

fall into my arms trapunto fall into my arms

it's all coming back in a rush

the kiss at the door that wasn't a kiss at the door
my scarlet sweater
the kiss just inside the door when the sky / clouds / ceiling fell in
accounting for trapunto's headache

he showed me his pain machine
his anti-pain machine
you stare into it and go off above your mind hypnotically
and the pain goes elsewhere

he took care the pain did not go into me

i brushed my hair

**2.**
much to my amazement
a tight elastic hairnet of pain (of stars)
was pulled down tightly over your skull

i shouldn't have told you what i was thinking
it was this

one could take the wind and wind it around missing persons all over the
    world and
find them
if one were on speaking terms with the wind
considering that the persons wanted to be found
(there will always be some who do not)

just before the bridge over the wide salty water there is a store
in which you can buy soda for missing persons and photographs of yourself
in a lobby machine
for them to remember you by

you can send these
via e-mail
all in one smooth transaction
except for the sodas

i am not speaking of persons in memory
or persons with orange hats or persons necessarily who
are not yet born
or are choosing not to be born or not to die

i am talking about the hairnet of pain that some people endure
that trapunto endured
the tight elastic dark blue navy blue hairnet of stars pulled down over the
head
bespeaking unendurable pain for some people
however beautiful

however beautiful the pain or the people

i never told him i dreamed the state color of new jersey was white
i believe he was thinking red that night

trapunto drank sherry and trapunto then smiled

red was a color that suited

# FLYING OVER THE HUDSON

they are cars and they
are small and they are people and
they are small and they are boats
and they are small

heaven is like that
that blue and sparking ocean
seen from the sky

when we fall in
it is cold
paralyzing
treacherous
filled with devils

don't set your life
on wanting to go there

# WONDERBENDER

this one's too pale that's too dark

we are discussing shades of yellow when you say please
stop saying you're sorry all the time and i say i'm sorry i don't usually
do that at all with other people but you you take things so hard and you say
if that's true it's my problem
if that's true

i have a strange antipathy to chlorinated smells

*circumference* means you must go all the way around

tuesday morning for the first time we saw the foxes
two of them trotting like tiny thoroughbred horses around the garden in the small snow
then fading back into the woods
we watched from your study—i with a mouthful of mouthwash waiting
to spit into the sink before i could say thank you thank you
for calling me

we had never seen the foxes before
not in this yard

the woodchucks are common, coyotes sometimes always the raccoons
and lots and lots of birds even wood-ducks
but never the foxes before tuesday no never

this will not mean much to you if you cannot put yourself in my shoes
or in my place with the mouthwash i should say
this will not mean much if you cannot understand fox-beauty or fox-light
or the secondary but also sharp joy later on in the day
of seeing their perfect pawprints near the newly transplanted star magnolia

something will grow in those pawprints in the spring

i have just read for the second time (though the first time i was small) *black beauty* and would like to write such a book

i write in first person because i am in first person

just like black beauty

in your voice on the recorded message there was a pale green jacket with a black lapel

in some senses it was a little off-the-shoulder
proving that you could change

i had not heard it the first time
but now it is a comfort

a tall man told my husband that he had called and checked out my story with a psychic
about his cat and it was true
in fact so many of my comments had been validated he could not remember all the details just then
the cat did not want to be just a tenant any more
she wanted to be part of the family
my husband forgot to tell me this right away
but when he did i was overjoyed

last night at the restaurant there were four of us and shiraz and lebanese
    food
delicious lentils
artichokes in tutus
and we had a nice time and then afterwards three of us went to the restroom
and i stayed behind to put on my coat
a man called my name from another table as i was walking out DIANE he
    said in a loud voice
i turned around
it was someone i'd known years ago in fact someone i'd championed in a

way and he'd
always been grateful
he was all smiley he had grown a beard
and a large stomach
we shook hands
he was sitting at a large round table with perhaps eight other people and he
began to introduce me around
his wife acknowledged me but the others did not seem interested
and yet this man was very happy to see me and it was a small but confusing
            boost
in an evening of sometimes confusing blackened lentils

*you must go all the way around*

the lentils weren't confusing exactly it was the conversation
but only at times
only in ways i can trace back to my childhood
when i began to hone an impending sense of something about to go wrong
with the air between parents
or not between parents exactly but between one of them at least
and the world

so i carry this seventh sense
in my bookbag
i carry this sense even without a bookbag it is tattooed on me
in the shape of a crocodile

right between my breasts
sometimes i put makeup over it
or hang a cloisonne pendant with a crocodile on it
just there

your desperation is kingpin
has gotten you nowhere
is the reason for oil-soaked shirts that will not wash clean
specks of white calcite on the green back stairs

*it's still dark so you can still speak*
*the dark soft light has crept into the garage*
*the car is waiting in its innocent darkness*
*to carry you anywhere anywhere*

this is the circumference not the diameter
i could explain it to you pretty well if you like by demonstrating with my hat

i am starting this month a day early
february
this is necessary because in january
i fell asleep at the most important part

i needed to go all the way the long way around

i tried to buy something made of titanium
but the mines were out of stock
i bought something made of organza
and watched a movie about asteroids which destroyed the earth by virtue
of their superior speed and beauty

organza

dental x-rays showing fields of swollen
wildflowers blue
chicory cornflower
in my mouth
much to the dentist's surprise
or at least he pretended

*wonder is bent at various times*
*quickly*
*and often invisibly*
*you don't realize till later*

*it has hurt you*

it has hurt you by omission by blocking out
the wonder the laughter the
amaze

over something so tiny it can hardly be real
like the miniature monkeys so small when they are born
they're smaller than your thumb

*i have seen pictures!*

speaking of monkeys the one in the beginning of *the lady from shanghai*
saddened me
leaping about on a string
love perhaps but a bound love
a little grey shirt and a teacup thimble-sized
and overall in any case i have to say i did not like
that lady from shanghai

*wonder when you lay there in that bed*
*all but dying*
*it was as if something else possessed you—it wasn't* not-you
*but you made sounds as if you had to go on*
*there was nothing i hadn't told you—it wasn't that kind of sad*
*it was as if something that tied my arm to my body was thinning to a thread*
*and i knew i would soon be a one-armed woman*
*for the rest of my life*

the miracles of wonder in that long-ago yard with no foxes but deer
small rabbits under the lawnchairs
bright orange and yellow nasturtium complete with ants
thick pears white dogwood johnny-jump-ups in the grass
a few stars replicated in birdsong dogbark kittensigh
your face as a child and wrapping your bee-stung neck in a white t-shirt
drenched in the dragonfly stream

did it help you?

i am sure now that there is no shame in being this way and that no one should deny it
and yet there were many moments even with wonder

when i was ashamed

i ate white crackers with no nutrition whatsoever
perhaps like communion wafers
i offered white wonder in the cup of my two small hands
right up to the stars
i wrote about your headband of pain the stars like a hairnet around your suffering

blue all blue
and as crystalline as the night the wonder kissed me

*please love me i knew you wonder would come along*
*sometime*
*it just took me a long time to find you i thought you were someone else*

*but you look just like me*
*you look just like me*
*you look just like me*

# ABOUT THE POET

Diane Wald was born in Paterson, NJ, and has lived in Massachusetts since 1972. She was the recipient of a two-year fellowship from the Fine Arts Work Center in Provincetown and has been awarded the Grolier Poetry Prize, the Denny Award, the Open Voice Award, the Anne Halley Prize, and a grant from the Artists Foundation (Massachusetts Council on the Arts). Her chapbooks are *Target of Roses, My Hat That Was Dreaming, Double Mirror, Improvisations on Titles of Works by Jean Dubuffet*, and *faustinetta, gegenschein, trapunto*, and she won the Green Lake Chapbook Award from Owl Creek Press. Wald's two previous poetry collections are *Lucid Suitcase* and *The Yellow Hotel.*

MORE TITLES FROM 1913 PRESS:

*Hg-the liquid*, Ward Tietz (2011)
*Home/Birth: A Poemic*, Arielle Greenberg & Rachel Zucker (2011)
*Ozalid*, Biswamit Dwibedy (2010)
*Sightings*, Shin Yu Pai (2007)
*Seismosis*, John Keene & Christopher Stackhouse (2006)
*1913 a journal of forms*, Issues 1-4

FORTHCOMING:

*1913 a journal of forms*, Issue 5 (2011)
*Big House/Disclosure*, Mendi & Keith Obadike (2011)
*Four Electric Ghosts*, Mendi & Keith Obadike (2011)
*The Transfer Tree*, Karena Youtz (2012)
*Conversities*, Dan Beachy-Quick & Srikanth Reddy (2012)

*1913 titles are distributed by Small Press Distribution www.spdbooks.org*
*& printed on recycled papers.*

GUILLAUME APOLLINAIRE

Memories are hunting horns whose sound dies on the wind.

ALCOOLS, 1913